JEHOVAH'S WITNESSES

WALTER MARTIN

BETHANY HOUSE PUBLISHERS
MINNEAPOLIS, MINNESOTA 55438
A Division of Bethany Fellowship, Inc.

First printing, 1957
Second printing, 1960
Third printing, 1961
Fourth printing, 1963
Fifth printing, 1964
Sixth printing, 1965
Seventh printing, 1966
Eighth printing, 1967
Ninth printing, 1968
Tenth printing, 1969
Eleventh printing, 1969
Twelfth printing, 1971
Thirteenth printing, 1971
Fourteenth printing, 1972
Fifteenth printing, 1972
Sixteenth printing, 1972
Seventeenth printing, 1973
Eighteenth printing, 1974
Nineteenth printing, 1974
Twentieth printing, 1977
Twenty-first printing, 1978
Twenty-second printing, 1979
Twenty-third printing, 1980
Twenty-fourth printing, 1981
Twenty-fifth printing, 1982
Twenty-sixth printing, 1984
Twenty-seventh printing, 1985
Twenty-eighth printing, 1987
Twenty-ninth printing, 1988

Jehovah's Witnesses
Walter R. Martin

ISBN 0-87123-270-7

Published by Bethany House Publishers
A Division of Bethany Fellowship, Inc.
6820 Auto Club Road, Minneapolis, Minnesota 55438

Printed in the United States of America

CONTENTS

PREFACE

The Watch Tower Bible and Tract Society, better known throughout the world as Jehovah's Witnesses, today presents a challenge to the Christian Church, which informed Christians ignore at the peril of millions of souls.

From meager beginnings in the 1880's to a membership of over 1,000,000, world-wide, the Watch Tower today sends forth its literature in a hundred languages, and continues to present a problem on every mission field where the testimony of the true Gospel of Christ is being impaired by the ever zealous disciples of "Pastor" Russell.

Since the publication of my book, *Jehovah of the Watch Tower* (Zondervan Publishing House, 1956, the 5th edition, revised and enlarged), the author has had many requests for a condensed presentation of the problem of Jehovah's Witnesses. It is hoped that this booklet may serve that purpose.

It should be realized at the outset that any thorough presentation of such a vast subject, involving as it does a tremendously zealous and vibrant organization, cannot be adequately covered in a booklet of this size. But I have attempted to deal with some of the important issues necessary to any sane evaluation of Jehovah's Witnesses today. With the prayer that the Lord of Glory may deign to bless this effort made in the defense of His Gospel, this work is offered.

WALTER R. MARTIN

Livingston, New Jersey

Chapter One

THE ANCESTRY OF JEHOVAH'S WITNESSES

Throughout the early history of the Christian Church, but especially in the first four centuries, the growing body of Christian believers later to become the Visible Church encountered both political and doctrinal opposition as they fought their way through the mazes of both Roman oppression and Greek mystical theology. However, none of these conflicts was more replete with dangers than that which the churches encountered with those who have been termed "the Arians of the fourth century" and who formed with the Roman oppressors a combination of the Church's two greatest enemies. These forces arrayed themselves against orthodox Christianity in all their power and cunning as both politically and doctrinally, the Arian heresy challenged the cornerstone of all Christendom and the authority of the Bible itself by denying with boldness the true Deity of Jesus Christ.

The origin of the controversy between those orthodox Christians who believed Jesus Christ to be truly God and truly man, and those called "Arians" who affirmed that He was merely the first and greatest of God's creatures created in time and elevated to the rank of "a god," began in the year 319 A.D. with Arius of Alexandria, a learned teacher and Presbyter of the Alexandrian church in Egypt.

Early in the history of the Christian Church, the rationalistic theology of Greece had begun to infiltrate itself into Christian doctrine, forever seeking a "reasonable" explanation to revelations and mysteries which were never intended to be fully understood outside of the mind of God (Col. 2:2, 3).

The most profound and mysterious of those revelations was unquestionably that of the blessed Trinity, with its three-Persons-in-one-God doctrine of Biblical pre-eminence. Seeking to explain this mystery away certain of the Greek-influenced theologians of the era criticized that part of the doctrine they believed most vulnerable, the identity and Nature of the second Person of the Trinity, Jesus Christ.

Prominent among these theologians was Lucian of Antioch, a leader in the Syrian church. This Greek-thinking mystic trained a whole group of potential enemies of orthodox Christianity and schooled them in the cleverness of dialectical theology. Devoted to the concept that "once the Son of God was not," Lucian stoutly challenged the eternal Deity of Christ but was unfortunately martyred for his radical views by over-zealous disciples of orthodoxy. However, even in death Lucian in a sense cursed his murderers, for his prized pupil lived to spread his teachings over all the Christian world and to split the Christian Church in a way that was not equaled until the Protestant Reformation. This pupil was the afore-mentioned Arius of Alexandria, a learned scholar but vain beyond description, whose unscriptural speculations set in motion the still living and powerful Arian heresy which threatened to destroy Christianity itself by undermining faith in our Lord Jesus Christ as the true Son of God; i.e. God the Son.

Briefly the Arian heresy can be summed up in this short proposition: (1) If God the Father gave birth to the Son, Jesus Christ who was born, has an origin of existence; (2) therefore, once the Son was not; (3) and therefore He was created out of nothing.

Arius arrived at this seemingly reasonable theory because not fully comprehending the Scriptures he sought to supply an answer for a question the Bible never completely answered; namely, how Christ is both God and man, never ceasing to be either yet true to each Nature.

In his first letter to the Corinthian church, St. Paul reveals glimpses of the mysterious relationship existing between the eternal God and His identical Son. In the first chapter of this letter Paul also declares that Christ is "the power and the wisdom of God," and John wrote that Jesus Christ was "the true God and eternal life" (I John 5:20). Arianism was mute before this revelation of truth, since if the Word or Reason of God did not always exist then the Father also has lacked true completeness; for were the Word not eternal then neither would the Father possess eternal wisdom and power, seeing that Christ is the fullness of both in Him. See also Hebrews 1:3, Titus 1:3, Colossians 2:9, John 1:1, etc.

Further than these facts the personal revelations which the Lord Jesus gave of His identity and equality with the Father were also mysteriously neglected by Arius and his followers, such as the eighth chapter of John's gospel, verse 58, wherein the Lord proclaimed Himself to be the "I am" of the Jehovah-Moses discourse as recorded in the book of Exodus (Ex. 3:14).

In the face of all this evidence Arius preferred to remain silent. He was also noncommittal when referred to the Scriptures where Jesus said, "All that the Father has is mine," and "I and my Father are one" (John 16:15; 10:30).

The question was, If Christ possesses all that the Father has, does He not possess His titles and thereby share His intrinsic deity also? The Arians again chose not to answer these embarrassing questions and were openly perplexed by the logic of the orthodox position, and the arguments advanced.

Time and time again as the Arian controversy raged Isaiah the prophet's words haunted the Arian debate: "For unto us a child is born, unto us a son is given: and the government shall be upon his shoulder: and his name shall be called Wonderful, Counsellor, The mighty God, The everlasting Father, The Prince of Peace" (Isa. 9:6). Arius dared not deny that the prophecy spoke of Jesus and ascribed to Him true deity, but he refused to answer the problem or to renounce his errors. Athanasius, the greatest enemy of Arianism, led the battle against the impious Arius, and at the Council of Nicaea which convened in Bithynia the summer of 325 A.D. he had the satisfaction of seeing the Arian theology officially condemned as heresy and its leaders excommunicated. Some 300 bishops banded together against the Arian minority of 30 (which dwindled at length to 18), as the Nicaean Council set its stamp of approval on what the Scriptures had always taught, that Jesus Christ is "the true God and eternal life" (I John 5:20).*

The Council of Nicaea drew a line once and for all between the theological double talk of the Arians and the straight pronouncement of the Bible. The Arians were willing to ascribe to Jesus Christ all the attributes and titles of His Father, except the one thing which alone could entitle Him to the identity of true deity, the equality of the Father's Substance or Nature. For if Christ be not of one Nature with His Father and the Holy Spirit, then He must be inferior to them and the unity of the Godhead becomes a hollow linguistic sham. We know however that the Christian Church has historically taught what the Scriptures declare; namely, that our Lord is Creator, Redeemer and Everlasting Sovereign, and that the Father Himself has decreed that one day at the name of Jesus every knee shall bend and every tongue shall confess that He is Lord to the glory of God the Father. (Phil. 2:10, 11). Certainly no one can say in retrospect that the Council of Nicaea solved the mystery of the Trinity or ended the Arian controversy, for it continued to flare for some years thereafter, but it did serve to reveal one important and wonderful truth which the Christian Church has held inviolate throughout the ensuing ages. This truth candidly states and affirms that there is *one* eternal God subsisting in *three* separate and distinct Persons: Father, Son and Holy Spirit; yet one in agreement of will, unity of Substance and equality of power,

* and later Chalcedon, 451 A.D.

"neither confounding the Persons nor dividing the Substance." This *one* Being Christendom universal adores and worships as alone true God and true man in Jesus Christ, who Himself personally commanded that we baptize "in the name of the Father, the Son and the Holy Spirit," and that these *three* in manifestation be worshiped as *one* in Personality and Nature (John 4:24) which is true unity, and the only real basis for Jehovah's being the *one* true and living God.

Today in the twentieth century the problem of the Trinity remains unsolved as it did in the times of Nicaea, and the rationalistic mind bent on analyzing God by the scientific method still rejects what it cannot term "reasonable." There are those persons who dishonor the Lord Jesus even as Arius did, when they say that Christ is "the first and greatest creation of Jehovah God and His active agent in creating all things." These same ones echo the old Arian heresy that "the Son is a mighty god but not Jehovah God." It is evident to see then that the Arian heresy still lives today, an old doctrine dressed up with new words and ideas but at heart still the blight of Christian orthodoxy under the new title of "The Watch Tower Bible and Tract Society," better known as Jehovah's Witnesses.

As we shall see, Jehovah's Witnesses in their desire to explain away the mysteries of Scripture, fail to see that if Christ is not God incarnate then they are polytheists, guilty of worshiping two gods, one Almighty as Jehovah, the other simply "a mighty god," Christ Jesus. However, God has said in His Word, and all informed students of Scripture know, that the Bible teaches that there is none other god but Jehovah and that He is the only true Deity. The prophet Isaiah reminds us, quoting the voice of the Lord ". . . before me there was no God formed, neither shall there be after me . . . I, even I, am the Lord; and beside me there is no saviour . . . I am the first, and I am the last; and beside me there is no God" (Isa. 43:10,11; 44:6; see also Isa. 42:8).

Faithful Christians today, then, as in the days of Arius, Athanasius and the Nicaean Council, reject the Arian rationalistic approach to theology which would rob God of His eternal relationship with Christ and the Holy Spirit, and accept instead the absolute pronouncement of the Lord Jesus Himself, "Before Abraham was, I Am" and ". . . if ye believe not that I Am, ye shall die in your sins" (John 8:24; 8:58).

THE MODERN ARIANS

As was previously noted, the Watch Tower Bible and Tract Society, the official organ of Jehovah's Witnesses, is the modern counterpart of the Arians of the fourth century and has adopted almost verbatim the Christological formula which Arius made popular.

Jehovah's Witnesses, the contemporary Arians of today, take their name from the 43rd chapter of Isaiah, verse 10, "Ye are my witnesses, saith the Lord, and my servant whom I have chosen: that ye may know and believe me, and understand that I am he: before me there was no God formed, neither shall there be after me." However, the present organization received the title "Jehovah's Witnesses" at the hand of the late Judge J. F. Rutherford at a convention held in 1931.

It is impossible in the space allotted for this booklet to do any more than sketch a brief modern history of Jehovah's Witnesses, but the following resumé is submitted in lieu of an exhaustive treatment of the subject. For those interested in a thorough presentation my book *Jehovah of the Watch Tower* (published by the Zondervan Publishing House, 1956) covers the subject extensively and is recommended if the reader is interested in historical data and a fuller exposition of Jehovah's Witnesses, their history and theology, etc.

HISTORY

The Watch Tower Bible and Tract Society came into existence in the year 1884 when Charles Taze Russell (1852-1916), better known as "Pastor" Russell, incorporated it under the title "Zion's Watch Tower Tract Society" at Pittsburgh, Pennsylvania. Charles Taze Russell was both the founder and first president of the Watch Tower Bible and Tract Society (1896) and the man who brought into existence the organization which is now known as Jehovah's Witnesses (Columbus, Ohio, 1931).

Born in Allegheny, Pennsylvania in 1852 Russell was reared a strict Congregationalist, but early in his religious experience the future "Pastor" revolted violently against the concept of hell and eternal punishment for the unsaved, a revolt which culminated in Russell's denial of practically every major doctrine of the Christian faith, from the Trinity and the deity of Christ to the bodily resurrection from the grave and the visible second advent of our Lord. Russell was a successful haberdasher in Pennsylvania, history tells us, but in the year 1870 at the tender age of 18 he organized a Bible class in Pittsburgh, and it was this class which in 1876 conferred upon him the title "Pastor." A man known for his zealous convictions, C. T. Russell invested a small fortune to promulgate his new found theological speculation and in 1879 he financed the publication of *Zion's Watch Tower*, the ancestor of today's *Watch Tower* magazine which has grown from its initial issue of 6,000 to the fabulous figure of approximately four million copies per month, as of May, 1960.

"Pastor" Russell was a controversial figure for many years, and a prolific writer, whose series of six volumes entitled "Studies in the Scriptures" (originally titled "Millennial Dawn") sold over twenty-five million copies and are still being distributed by some of his followers to this day. It is needless to go into the scandals which characterized the life of "Pastor" Russell, since I have already chronicled them in detail in my book,[1] but suffice it to say that he was a proven perjurer, a man of questionable moral character, an out-of-context paraphraser of Scripture, and a sworn enemy of evangelical Christianity, whose followers "Jehovah's Witnesses" of today have never ceased to emulate where theology is concerned.

Today the Watch Tower Bible and Tract Society operates a printing plant in Brooklyn, New York (its headquarters), which prints *Watch Tower* literature in over 100 languages and distributes it in more than 140 lands and on every foreign mission field throughout the world. The *Watch Tower* also owned until recently its own radio station (WBBR — 1330 kcs, 5000 watts) which spread the Russellite gospel throughout New York, New Jersey, Connecticut, etc., month in and month out tirelessly peddling a slightly revised edition of the theology of its founder, Charles Taze Russell.

Jehovah's Witnesses have many times denied that they are still following "Pastor" Russell's theology. However in the April 8, 1951 edition of *Awake* magazine they finally played out enough "printed rope," figuratively speaking, to hang themselves. In this edition the *Watch Tower* denied categorically that it is following Russell's teaching. Yet it can be shown from their own current publications that Jehovah's Witnesses have never stopped following Russell (see chapters 2 and 3) — an unpleasant fact the *Watch Tower* would very much like to forget!

On October 31, 1916 aboard a transcontinental train, near Pampa, Texas, the first president of the Watch Tower Bible and Tract Society, "Pastor" Charles Taze Russell passed from the earthly scene, wrapped according to his last wishes in a bed sheet resembling a Roman toga! With the death of Russell the Watch Tower Board of Directors scrambled for control of the now vacant throne and various splits ensued as

1 See *Jehovah of the Watch Tower*, Chapter I.

the result of the "election" of Judge J. F. Rutherford as successor to the "Pastor."

Joseph Franklin Rutherford took over the organization bequeathed to him by "Pastor" Russell and with marvelous business acumen, tremendous vitality, and an insatiable drive for accomplishment pyramided the "Pastor's" heretofore limited operation into a multi-million dollar cult of zealous people who spend most of their time negating the beliefs of others and openly attacking the sacred truths of historic Christianity. It is this attitude which makes booklets like this necessary. If this charge seems severe the reader is referred to a statement made by Mr. Roger Baldwin, quoted in the November 2, 1946, issue of *Collier's* magazine concerning the growth and development of the Watch Tower Bible and Tract Society. It should be noted that Mr. Baldwin is no friend of orthodox Christianity; therefore his criticism of the *Watch Tower* based upon a thorough knowledge of their contemporary activities is most significant. Said Mr. Baldwin, of the American Civil Liberties Union, commenting upon Jehovah's Witnesses' numerous trials before our courts: "By contesting in the courts every restriction on them these Jehovah's Witnesses . . . have served the cause of their fellow men, *whom they abhor.*" Note that although Mr. Baldwin recognized the worth of Jehovah's Witnesses' campaigns in the courts of our land, nevertheless he has not been deceived by the *Watch Tower*, for he goes on to state that the Witnesses "abhor" or hate their fellow men whose cause they have in a sense served by test cases on civil liberties.

In addition to this the *Watch Tower* has never ceased to pour from its presses direct attacks upon Christianity, both Roman Catholic and Protestant, and in the words of Stanley High, noted editor and author, writing in the *Saturday Evening Post* for September 14, 1940: "Jehovah's Witnesses hate everybody and try to make it mutual."

For those who wish further documentation on this point, we refer you to the *Watch Tower* of December, 1951, pages 731 to 733, where the Witnesses are displayed at their intolerant worst. Should additional information be needed the October 1, 1952, issue of the *Watch Tower*, pages 596 to 604, counsels the Witnesses to manifest "pure" hatred for the enemies of the Theocracy. All religions by definition qualify here.

This attitude of hatred on the part of the Witnesses was fostered by J. F. Rutherford and continues to be promulgated under the direction of Nathan H. Knorr, present president of the *Watch Tower*. Indeed Jehovah's Witnesses seem to thrive on antagonism and their genius for stirring up conflicts between peoples of different religious backgrounds. It was J. F. Rutherford, incidentally, who at one time broadcast over 403 radio stations coast-to-coast, as well as over a Canadian hook-up, and first counseled Jehovah's Witnesses to make hate pay off. It is an easily verifiable fact that the Witnesses have heeded the counsel of the Judge who termed all religions "a snare and a racket," despite the fact that he occupied a mansion (Beth Sarim) outside San Diego, California (allegedly appraised at $60,000)[2] for some years and justified his occupancy of that palatial edifice on the ground that he was only taking care of the premises until Abraham, Isaac, David, etc., returned to earth to commence the millennial reign![3] In the light of this fact and many others it is no wonder that many critics of Jehovah's Witnesses have questioned the Judge's sincerity, not to mention the fact that in a supposedly democratic corporation, the Watch Tower Bible and Tract Society, he ruled said *Watch Tower* with an iron hand until his death January 8, 1942, and cracked the proverbial whip over the heads of the entire *Watch Tower* Board of Directors who served

[2] Some estimates run as high as $75,000.
[3] See "Salvation" — J. F. Rutherford, p. 311; "Consolation," Nov. 1941; also Stroup, H. H., *The Jehovah's Witnesses*, Columbia University Press, 1945, p. 42.

as a convenient whipping boy for his honor's frequent tirades of anger directed against all those who dared to question his reign in the Society. (See H. H. Stroup, *The Jehovah's Witnesses,* Columbia University Press, 1945, pp. 25, 26).
pp. 25, 26).

The history of Jehovah's Witnesses then, tracing their theological ancestry from the days of Arius of Alexandria through Charles Taze Russell, J. F. Rutherford and Nathan H. Knorr, reveals a checkered eclectic pattern of theological perversion, amply seasoned with sincerity and hawked to an unwary public by a zealous group of badly misled persons. These people have been hypnotized by the *Watch Tower* into what ex-Witness W. J. Schnell describes as a "zombie-like" state, and they proffer Russellite mythology to a lost world that in reality needs the Gospel of Jesus Christ, *not* Russellism in any form.

Chapter Two

THE WATCH TOWER CHAMELEON

The Watch Tower Bible and Tract Society possesses among other things a remarkable gift, the ability to change its appearance in such a way as to mislead many persons into believing that it is no longer following the teachings of its first president and founder, Charles Taze Russell. The reason for this chameleon-like activity is the fact that Russell's unsavory past is a skeleton which has been hidden in the Watch Tower's closet for the last forty years and the Russell-ites are most eager to keep the bones from rattling too loudly.

A chameleon as everyone knows, is a small lizard which has the facility of rapidly changing its color thereby adapting itself to almost any color shade or surface upon which it is placed; and how true this has been, historically speaking, of the Watch Tower!

In the early days of its development, before the Watch Tower was "born" as an organization, Charles Taze Russell, its founder, called himself and his followers "Bible Students." As the organization began to grow, however, Russell found it necessary to incorporate under an official name. This young Russell did, in 1879, when he founded "Zion's Watch Tower Magazine" (a magazine which is today known as "The Watch Tower Announcing Jehovah's Kingdom") a small organ which was to become the mouthpiece of his new organization. In the year 1884, as stated in chapter I, Russell incorporated "Zion's Watch Tower Tract Society" at Pittsburgh, Pennsylvania, an organization later supplanted by the Watch Tower Bible and Tract Society. Moving from the area of Allegheny or Pittsburgh in Pennsylvania, to Brooklyn, N. Y. Russell continued to circulate his teachings under the title of "The Millennial Dawn," and published six books entitled "The Millennial Dawn Series" a name he later changed to "Studies in the Scriptures," because many prominent clergymen unmasked his "Studies" for the perversions that they were. While residing in Brooklyn, Russell organized what he termed "The People's Pulpit" and later the "International Bible Students" all pseudonyms for the real name of this cult, the name which today brands Jehovah's Witnesses as "Russellism" even as it did in Russell's day. In the year 1931 in Columbus, Ohio, 15 years after Russell's death, the reader will recall Judge J. F. Rutherford, successor to "Pastor" Russell dubbed the new organization "Jehovah's Witnesses," and they have remained such to this day. However, it is a fairly simple historical matter to establish the fact that they have accommodated themselves to whatever environment surrounded them, and for many years hid their true identity as they still do in some instances.

Jehovah's Witnesses as previously mentioned have for many years maintained that they are not following "Pastor" Russell. But as we shall see in a moment such a claim is demonstrably false. In parallel columns listed below we have tabulated the teachings of Charles Taze Russell and the doctrines of Jehovah's Witnesses, juxtaposed so that the unbiased reader may study for himself actual quotations in context from the writings of Russell and Jehovah's Witnesses, the study of which we believe will convince any open-minded individual that the two systems are practically identical, irrespective of Jehovah's Witnesses' loud protests to the contrary.

THE TEACHINGS OF CHARLES TAZE RUSSELL OR "RUSSELLISM"

I. TRIUNE GODHEAD

1. This view [the Trinity]¹ suited well the dark ages it helped to produce (*Studies in the Scriptures*, Vol. V, p. 166).

2. This . . . theory is as unscriptural as it is unreasonable (*Op. cit.*, Vol. V, p. 166).

3. . . . If it were not for the fact that this trinitarian nonsense was drilled into us from earliest infancy and the fact that it is so soberly taught in Theological Seminaries by gray haired professors, . . . nobody would give it a moment's serious consideration (*Op. cit.*, Vol. V, p. 166).

4. How the great adversary [Satan]² ever succeeded in fostering it [The Triune Godhead]² upon the Lord's people to bewil-

THE DOCTRINES OF JEHOVAH'S WITNESSES

I. TRIUNE GODHEAD (Speaking of John 1:1-3)

1. Does this mean that Jehovah God (Elohim) and the . . . Son are two persons but at the same time one God and members of a so-called "trinity" or "triune god"? When religion so teaches it violates the Word of God, wrests the Scriptures to the destruction of those who are misled, and insults God-given intelligence and reason (*The Truth Shall Make You Free*, p. 45).

2. Only the religious "trinitarians" are presumptuous enough to claim, without Scripture basis, that two other persons are equal with Jehovah God; but Jesus does not himself claim to be one of such persons (*The Kingdom Is at Hand*, p. 507).

3. The Trinity doctrine was not conceived by Jews or the early Christians (*Let God Be True*, p. 92).

4. The obvious conclusion, therefore, is that Satan is the originator of the Trinity doctrine (*Let God Be True*, ed., 1946, p. 82).

¹ Brackets are ours.
² Brackets are ours.

der and mystify them and render much of the Word of God of none effect is the real mystery... (*Op. cit.*, Vol. V, p. 166).

II. THE DEITY OF JESUS CHRIST

1. . . . Our Lord Jesus Christ is a god . . . still the united voice of the Scriptures must emphatically assert that there is but one Almighty God, the Father of all (*Studies in the Scriptures*, Vol. V, p. 55).

2. . . . The Logos [Christ][3] himself was "the beginning of the creation of God" (*Op. cit.*, Vol. V, p. 86).

3. Our Redeemer existed as a spirit being before he was made flesh and dwelt amongst men. At that time, as well as subsequently, he was properly known as "a god" —a mighty one (*Op. cit.*, Vol. V, p. 84).

4. As chief of the angels and next to the Father, he [Christ][3]

II THE DEITY OF JESUS CHRIST

1. . . . The true Scriptures speak of God's Son, the Word, as "a god." He is a "mighty God," but not "the almighty God, who is Jehovah" — Isaiah 9:6 (*The Truth Shall Make You Free*, p. 47).

2. At the time of his beginning of life he was created by the everlasting God, Jehovah, without the aid or instrumentality of any mother. In other words, he was the first and direct creation of Jehovah God. . . . He was the start of God's creative work. He was not an incarnation in flesh but was flesh, a human Son of God, a perfect man, no longer a spirit, although having a spiritual or heavenly post and background (*The Kingdom Is at Hand*, pp. 46, 47, 49).

3. This One was not Jehovah God, but was existing in the form of God . . . he was a spirit person . . . he was a mighty one although not Almighty as Jehovah God is; . . . he was a god, but not the Almighty God, who is Jehovah (*Let God Be True*, pp. 34, 35).

4. Being the only begotten Son of God . . . the Word would

[3] Brackets are ours.

was known as the Archangel (highest angel or messenger), whose name, Michael, signifies, "Who as God" or "God's Representative" (*Op. cit.*, Vol. V, p. 84).

be a prince among all other creatures. In this office he [Christl[4] bore another name in heaven, which name is "Michael." . . . Other names were given to the Son in the course of time (*The Truth Shall Make You Free*, p. 49).

III. THE RESURRECTION OF CHRIST

1. . . . Our Lord was put to death in flesh, but was made alive in spirit; he was put to death a man, but was raised from the dead a spirit being of the highest order of the divine nature: (*Studies in the Scriptures*, Vol. V, p. 453).

2. . . . It could not be that the man Jesus is the second Adam, the new father of the race instead of Adam; for the Man Jesus is dead, forever dead . . . (*Op. cit.*, Vol. V, p. 454).

3. . . . . He [Christ][4] instantly created and assumed such a body of flesh and such clothing as he saw fit for the purpose intended (*Op cit.*, Vol. II, p. 127).

4. Our Lord's human body . . . did not decay or corrupt . . . whether it was dissolved into gases or whether it is still pre-

III. THE RESURRECTION OF CHRIST

1. . . . In his resurrection he was no more human. He was raised as a spirit creature . . . (*The Kingdom Is at Hand*, p. 258).

2. . . . Jehovah God raised him from the dead, not as a human son, but as a mighty immortal spirit son. . . . So the King Christ Jesus was put to death in the flesh and was resurrected an invisible spirit creature (*Let God Be True*, pp. 43, 122).

3. Therefore the bodies in which Jesus manifested himself to his disciples after his return to life were not the body in which he was nailed to the tree. They were merely materialized for the occasion, resembling on one or two occasions the body in which he died . . . (*The Kingdom Is at Hand*, p. 259).

4. The Firstborn one from the dead was not raised out of the grave a human creature, but he was raised a spirit (*Let God Be*

[4] Brackets are ours.

served somewhere . . . no one knows (*Op cit.*, Vol. II, p. 129).

True, p. 272).

IV. The Physical Return of Christ

1. And in like manner as he went away (quietly, secretly, so far as the world was concerned, and unknown except to his followers), so in this manner, he comes again (*Studies in the Scriptures*, Vol. II, p. 154).

2. [Russell's idea of what Christ is saying, and his teaching on the matter.]
. . . He comes to us in the early dawn of the Millennial Day. Jesus seems to say . . . "Learn that I am a spirit being, no longer visible to human sight" (*Op. cit.*, Vol. II, p. 191).

3. He [Christ][5] does not come in the body of his humiliation, a human body which he took for the suffering of death . . . but in his glorious spiritual body . . . (*Op. cit.*, Vol. II, p. 108).

V. The Existence of Hell or a Place of Conscious Torment After Death

1. Many have imbibed the erroneous idea that God placed our race on trial for life with the alternative of eternal torture, whereas nothing of the kind is even

IV. The Physical Return of Christ

1. Christ Jesus comes, not as a human but as a glorious spirit creature (*Let God Be True*, p. 185).

2. Since no earthly men have ever seen the Father . . . neither will they see the glorified Son . . . (*Op. cit.*, p. 186).

3. It is a settled Scriptural truth, therefore, that human eyes will not see him at his second coming, neither will he come in a fleshly body.

4. . . . . Christ Jesus came to the Kingdom in A.D. 1914, but unseen to men (*The Truth Shall Make You Free*, pp. 295, 300).

V. The Existence of Hell or a Place of Conscious Torment After Death

1. . . . The Bible hell is the tomb, the grave . . . (*Let God Be True*, p. 72).

---

[5] Brackets are ours.

hinted at in the penalty (*Studies in the Scriptures*, Vol. I, p. 127).

2. Eternal torture is nowhere suggested in the Old Testament Scriptures, and only a few statements in the New Testament can be so misconstrued as to appear to teach it (*Op. cit.*, Vol. I, p. 128).

2. . . . God-dishonoring doctrine . . . (*Op. cit.*, p. 79).

3. The doctrine of a burning hell where the wicked are tortured eternally after death cannot be true . . . (*Op. cit.*, p. 80).

One of the most distressing traits manifested in the literature and teachings of Jehovah's Witnesses is their seemingly complete disregard for historical facts and dependable literary consistency. At the same time, however, they condemn all religious opponents as "enemies of God"[6] and perpetrators of what they term "a racket"[7]

For some time now the author has been considerably disturbed by Jehovah's Witnesses' constant denial of any theological connection whatsoever with "Pastor" Charles T. Russell, their admitted founder and first president of the Watch Tower Bible and Tract Society. Since Russell was long ago proven to be a perjurer under oath, a sworn adversary of historic Christianity, and a scholastic fraud, it is obvious why the Witnesses seek to avoid his influence and memory whenever possible. Be that as it may, however, some light should be thrown on the repeated self-contradictions which are committed by the Witnesses, in their zeal to justify their position and the ever-wavering doctrines to which they hold. It is our contention that they are following the basic teachings of Charles T. Russell in relation to many Biblical doctrines which he denied, and from their own publication we shall document this accusation.

In their eagerness to repudiate the charge of "Russellism," the Witnesses dogmatically say: ". . . but who is preaching the teaching of Pastor Russell? *Certainly not* Jehovah's Wit-

[6] J. F. Rutherford, *Deliverance*, p. 91; also *Religion*, pp. 263, 268.
[7] *Religion*, pp. 88, 104, 133, 137, 140, 141, etc.

nesses! They cannot be accused of following him, for they *neither quote him as an authority nor publish nor distribute his writings.*"[8] This is the statement of the Witnesses' magazine. Now let us compare this with history, and the truth will be plainly revealed.

Historically, Jehovah's Witnesses have quoted "Pastor" Russell numerous times since his death in 1916. The following is a token sample of what we can produce as concrete evidence. In 1923, seven years after the "Pastor's" demise, Judge J. F. Rutherford, then heir apparent to the Russellite throne, wrote a booklet some fifty-odd pages in length, entitled *World Distress — Why and the Remedy.* In this informative treatise, the new president of The Watch Tower Bible and Tract Society and the International Bible Students quoted "Pastor" Russell no less than *sixteen* separate times; referred to his books, *Studies in the Scriptures,* over *twelve* times; and devoted *six* pages at the end of the booklet to advertising these same volumes. Further than this, in a fifty-seven-page pamphlet published in 1925 and entitled *Comfort for the People,* by the same Rutherford, "his honor," in true Russellite character defines clergymen as "dumb dogs (D.D.)," proceeds to quote "Pastor" Russell's prophetical chronology (1914 A.D.),[9] and then sums up his tirade against Christendom universal by recommending Russell's writings in *four* pages of advertisements at the rear of the book.

The dark specter of historical facts thus begins to creep across the previously happy picture of a "Russell-free"[10] movement. But let us further consult history. In the year 1927,

---

[8] *Awake,* May 8, 1951, p. 26.

[9] Jehovah's Witnesses still hold to this today and teach it as dogma.

[10] In recent years, Jehovah's Witnesses have been forced openly to acknowledge Russell owing to the effect of my book *Jehovah of the Watch Tower,* which gave the true history of Russell's infamous doings, thus necessitating an answer from the Witnesses, even if it was an unreliable one in many respects and highly colored. The historical series was run in *The Watch Tower* for some months and was entitled "A Modern History of Jehovah's Witnesses." It was a very weak apologetic.

The Watch Tower Bible and Tract Society published Judge
Rutherford's "great" literary effort entitled *Creation,* which
was circulated into the millions of copies, and in which this
statement appeared concerning "Pastor" Russell:

> The second presence of Christ dates from about 1874.
>
> From that time forward many of the truths long obscured by
> the enemy began to be restored to the honest Christian.
>
> As William Tyndale was used to bring the Bible to the at-
> tention of the people, so the Lord used Charles T. Russell to
> bring to th∍ attention of the people an understanding of the
> Bible, particularly of those truths that had been taken away by
> the machinations of the Devil and his agencies. Because it was
> the Lord's due time to restore these truths, he used Charles
> T. Russell to write and publish books known as *Studies in the
> Scriptures* by which the great fundamental truths of the divine
> plan are clarified. Satan has done his best to destroy these
> books because they *explain* the Scriptures. Even as Tyndale's
> Version of the Bible was destroyed by the clergy, so the clergy
> in various parts of the earth have gathered together thousands
> of volumes of *Studies in the Scriptures* and burned them pub-
> licly. But such wickedness has only served to advertise the
> truth of the divine plan.

Please consider, if you will, this statement by the then
president of the Jehovah's Witnesses organization. Rutherford plainly quotes Russell and his writings as authoritative
material, yet *The Watch Tower* today claims *that Jehovah's
Witnesses are free* from the taint of "Russellism"!

Concluding this brief historical synopsis of the Watch
Tower Society's past, we quote the grand finale of J. F.
Rutherford's funeral oration over the prostrate remains of
"dear Brother Russell" who, according to the floral sign by
his casket, remained "faithful unto death." Said the Judge:
"Our brother sleeps not in death, but was instantly changed
from the human to the divine nature, and is now forever with
the Lord." This episode in Jehovah's Witnesses' history is cited
for its uniqueness, to show the adoration in which Russell was

once held by the theological ancestors of those who deny his influence today.

Leaving the past history of the Witnesses, we shall now answer those who say: "The Society may have quoted him in the past, but that was before Judge Rutherford's death. We do not do it now, and after all, didn't we say 'neither quote . . . publish . . . nor distribute his writings'? This is in the *present* tense, not the past." This would, we agree, be a splendid refutation of our claims if it were true, but as we shall now conclusively prove, it is not! Not only did Jehovah's Witnesses quote the "Pastor" as an authority in the past, before Rutherford's death in 1942, but they have done it right up until 1953, eleven years *after* his death.

In the July 15, 1950, edition of *The Watch Tower* (p. 216), the Witnesses quoted "Pastor" Russell as an authority regarding his chronology on the 2,520-year-reign of the Gentiles, which reign allegedly ended, according to his calculations (and Jehovah's Witnesses), in A.D. 1914. To make it even a more hopeless contradiction, they listed as their source, *The Watch Tower* of 1880, of which "Pastor" Russell was editor-in-chief! Now if they "do not consider his writings authoritative and do not circulate them," why (1) publish his chronology, (2) quote his publication as evidence and (3) admit his teachings on this vital point in their theology?

To shatter any misconception as to their literary shortcomings, we refer the interested reader to a pamphlet published by The Watch Tower, entitled *Jehovah's Witnesses, Communists or Christians?* (1953). Throughout the major content of this comparatively recent propaganda, Jehovah's Witnesses defend the thesis that they are not Communists (which they are not), but, in their zeal to prove "their skirts clean," they quote "Pastor" Russell's writings no less than *five times*, refer to them with apparent pride *twice* (pp. 4, 5), and even mention *two* of his best-known works, *The Plan of the Ages* (1886), and *The Battle of Armageddon* (1897). Further than this, *The Watch Tower* of October 1, 1953, quotes "Pastor" Russell's *Studies in the Scriptures* (Vol. IV, p. 554) (and Judge Rutherford's *Vindication* [Vol. II, p. 311] —), convincing evidence indeed that *The Watch Tower* still follows the Russellite theology of its much denied founder. All this despite the fact that they say, in their own words, "Jehovah's Witnesses . . . neither quote him [Russell] as an authority nor publish nor distribute his writings" (*Awake*, p. 26).

Through a careful perusal of these facts, it is a simple matter to determine that Jehovah's Witnesses have never stopped being "Russellites," no matter how loudly they proclaim the opposite. To those who are enmeshed in The Watch Tower's web, we can only say that you are *not* following a "new" Theocratic organization, you are following the old teachings of Charles Taze Russell, a bitter antagonist of historic Christianity, who has bequeathed to you a gospel of spiritual confusion. To those who are contemplating becoming members of The Watch Tower Society, we ask you to weigh the evidence found here and elsewhere[11] and to judge for yourselves whether it is wiser to trust the plain teachings of the Scripture and the guidance of the Holy Spirit and the Christian Church or to cast your lot with a group of zealous but misled people who are "blindly leading the blind down the broad way which leads to destruction." These persons it should be remembered have abandoned practically every cardinal doctrine of Biblical Christianity for the dogmatic doctrinal deviations of Charles Taze Russell and J. F. Rutherford. In the light of Holy Scripture, however, Russellism is shown to be a snare from whose grip only Jesus Christ can deliver.

[11] *Jehovah of the Watch Tower*, Martin and Klann (Grand Rapids: Zondervan Publishing House, 1956), Chapter I.

CHAPTER THREE

CARDINAL TEACHINGS OF THE WATCH TOWER

The theology of Jehovah's Witnesses is eclectic by nature, that is, it is by no means original, being the product of the speculative interpretations of Russell and Rutherford, who themselves borrowed liberally from many sources in constructing the beliefs which now constitute the basic teachings of the Watch Tower Bible and Tract Society.

While it is true that some of the teachings of the Watch Tower (anti-blood transfusion, the invisible "presence" of Christ, the 1914 prophetic chronology, etc.) can probably be considered peculiar to Russellism, nevertheless, the basic theology of the Watch Tower is borrowed. One need only study church history, especially the history of the early church to realize as stated earlier that the Jehovah's Witnesses of today are modern followers of the great Arian heresy, promulgated in the third century of the Christian Church. "Pastor" Russell copied his Christology from Arius of Alexandria, a learned Presbyter who denied categorically the deity of Jesus Christ. Arius taught that our Lord was a created being, the first and greatest creation of God who was elevated to the rank of "a God" due to his perfect life of obedience as a man and the fact that he was the first creature God made.

To outline fully all of the theological deviations inherent in the Watch Tower's system of doctrines is quite beyond the scope of this booklet. However, we have chosen to present under separate headings quotations from primary Watch Tower sources devoid of any comment by the author which the interested reader can peruse and evaluate for himself, and after reasonable study decide whether or not the Watch Tower Society can rightfully be classified as a Christian sect.

All of the following quotations are taken from publications of the Watch Tower Bible and Tract Society and remain true to the context from which they have been selected. Should any doubt the authenticity of these excerpts from bona fide Watch Tower publications, he is at liberty to obtain the volumes in question and compare the quotations as we have presented them with the originals as they appear in the respective Watch Tower volumes.

I and II. The Triune Godhead and the Deity of Jesus Christ

(Their definition of what they think the "religionists" teach).

1. *Definition*: "The doctrine, in brief, is that there are three gods in one: God the Father, God the Son, and God the Holy Ghost, all three equal in power, substance and eternity" (*"Let God Be True,"* p. 81, edition 1946).

2. The justice of God would not permit that Jesus, as a ransom, be *more* than a perfect man; and certainly *not* the Supreme God Almighty in the flesh (*op. cit.*, p. 87).

3. Some insist that Jesus when on earth was both God and man in completeness. *This theory is wrong,*[1] however . . . It is also easy to see that Jesus *could not*[1] be part God and part man, because that would be more than the law required; hence divine justice could not accept such a ransom (*The Harp of God*, J. F. Rutherford, pp. 101, 128).

4. The Holy Spirit is not a person, and is therefore not one of the Gods of the Trinity (Ref. *Reconciliation*, J. F. Rutherford, p. 115). (Also *Let God Be True*, p. 81, par. 1).

5. The "Trinity" doctrine was not conceived by Jesus or the early Christians (*op. cit.*, p. 92).

---

[1] Emphasis is ours.

6. The plain truth is that this is another of *Satan's*[2] attempts to keep the God-fearing person from learning the truth of Jehovah and His Son Christ Jesus (*op. cit.*, p. 93).

7. The obvious conclusion therefore is that *Satan*[2] is the originator of the "trinity doctrine" (*op. cit.*, p. 82).

III AND IV. THE RESURRECTION OF CHRIST AND THE ATONEMENT

1. This first-born one [Christ][2] from the dead was not[2] *raised* out of the grave *a human creature* but *he was raised a spirit* (*Let God Be True*, p. 272, edition 1946).

2. He was put to death a man, but was raised from the dead a *spirit being* of the highest order of the divine nature . . . *the man* Jesus is dead, forever dead (Russell, *op. cit.*, V, pp. 453, 454).

3. So the King Christ Jesus was put to death in the flesh and was resurrected an invisible spirit creature (*Let God Be True*, p. 122).

4. The "ransom for all" given by "the man Christ Jesus" *does not give or guarantee everlasting life* or blessing to any man (Russell, *Studies in the Scriptures*, I, p. 150).

5. That which is redeemed is *that which was lost,* namely, perfect human life with all its rights and earthly prospects (*Let God Be True*, p. 96).

V AND VI. THE RETURN OF CHRIST AND HUMAN GOVERNMENT

1. Christ Jesus came, not as human, but as a glorious spirit creature (*Let God Be True*, p. 185).

2. Some wrongfully expect a literal fulfillment of the symbolic statements of the Bible. Such hope to see the glorified Jesus coming seated on a white cloud where every human eye will see him . . . Since no earthly men have

[2] Emphasis is ours; brackets are ours.

ever seen the Father . . . neither will they see the glorified Son (*op. cit.,* p. 186).

3. It does not mean that he [Christ][8] is on the way or has promised to come, but that he has already arrived (*op. cit.,* pp. 187, 188).

4. Jehovah's Witnesses do not salute the flag of any nation (*op. cit.,* p. 234).

5. Any national flag is a symbol or image of the sovereign power of that nation (*op. cit.,* p. 235).

6. All such likenesses (symbols of a national power, eagle, sun, lion, etc.) are forbidden by Exodus 20:2-6 (the commandment of idolatry) (*op. cit.,* p. 235).

7. Therefore, no witness of Jehovah, who ascribes salvation *only* to Him, may salute any flag of any nation without a violation of Jehovah's commandment against idolatry as stated in His Word—I John 5:21 (*op. cit.,* p. 236).

VII AND VIII. THE EXISTENCE OF HELL AND ETERNAL PUNISHMENT

1. It is so plain that the Bible Hell is the tomb, the grave, that even an honest little child can understand it, but not the religious theologians (*op. cit.,* pp. 72, 73).

2. And now, who is responsible for this God-dishonoring doctrine, and what is his purpose? *The promulgator of it is Satan Himself;* and his purpose in introducing it has been to frighten the people away from studying the Bible and to make them hate God (*op. cit.,* p. 79).

3. The doctrine of a burning hell where the wicked are tortured eternally after death cannot be true, mainly for four reasons: (1) Because it is wholly unscriptural; (2) Because it is unreasonable; (3) Because it is contrary to God's love; and (4) Because it is repugnant to justice (*op cit.,* p. 80).

The summation of the whole matter then is a clear-cut denial by Jehovah's Witnesses of these great Scriptural doctrines especially the last mentioned. This great hatred of

[8] Emphasis is ours; brackets are ours.

God's justice undoubtedly stems from the founder of the organization, Russell, and its chief propagandist, Rutherford, both of whom campaigned relentlessly against the eternal justice of God in the form of conscious separation and torment as revealed in God's Word. Rutherford we believe voiced the conviction of every true Jehovah's Witness on this doctrinal truth when he said —

"Eternal torture is void of the principle of love; God is love: A Creator that would torture his creatures eternally would be a *fiend*[4] and not a God of Love" (quoted from *World Distress* by J. F. Rutherford, p. 40).

IX. SATAN — THE DEVIL

1. The Devil was not always the Devil. There was a time when he enjoyed a high position in God's family. He was a spirit son of God whose name was Lucifer (*Let God Be True*, p. 47).

2. He rebelled against the Theocratic arrangement (*op. cit.*, p. 55).

3. The ultimate end of Satan is complete annihilation (*op. cit.*, p. 55).

X AND XI. MAN THE SOUL: HIS NATURE AND DESTINY

1. . . . man is a combination of two things, namely, the "dust of the ground" and "the breath of life." The combining of these two things (or elements) produced a living soul or creature called man (*Let God Be True*, p. 59, edition 1946).

2. Thus we see that the claim of religionists that man has an immortal soul, and therefore differs from the beast, is not Scriptural (*op. cit.*, pp. 59, 60).

3. Thus it is seen that the serpent (the Devil) is the one who originated the doctrine of the inherent immortality of the soul (*op. cit.*, p. 66).

[4] Emphasis is ours.

XII. THE KINGDOM OF HEAVEN (A HEAVENLY ONE)

1. Who, and how many, are able to enter the Kingdom? Revelation limits the number to 144,000 that become a part of the Kingdom and stand on Mount Zion — Revelation 14:1, 3; 7:4-8 (*Let God Be True*, p. 121).

2. He (Christ) went to prepare a heavenly place for his associate members, the "body of Christ," for they too will be invisible creatures (*op. cit.*, p. 123).

3. The undefeatable purpose of Jehovah God to establish a righteous kingdom in these last days was fulfilled A.D. 1914 (*op. cit.*, p. 128).

4. Even the Creator so loved the New World that he gave his only begotten Son to be its King — John 3:16 (*op. cit.*, p. 128).

5. If it is to be a heavenly Kingdom who will be the subjects of its rule? In the invisible realm angelic hosts, myriads of them, will serve as faithful messengers of the King. And on earth the faithful men of ancient times, being resurrected, will be "princes in all the earth" (Psalm 45:16; Isaiah 32:1) . . . Also the "great multitude" of Armageddon survivors will continue to "serve him day and night" (Rev. 7:9-17). In faithfulness these will "multiply, and fill the earth" and their children will become obedient subjects of the Higher Powers. And finally the "unjust" ones that are resurrected, in proving their integrity, will joyfully submit themselves to Theocratic rule (Acts 24:15). Those who prove rebellious or who turn unfaithful during Satan's loosing at the end of Christ's thousand year reign will be annihilated with Satan the Devil — Revelation 20:7-15 (*op. cit.*, pp. 123, 124).

Jehovah's Witnesses have spoken for themselves in the foregoing quotations presented from their own publications. There cannot therefore be any doubt that they have been fairly represented relative to the particular areas of doctrine upon which the foregoing quotations bear.

CHAPTER FOUR

A REFUTATION OF THE TEACHINGS OF
JEHOVAH'S WITNESSES

We have seen in the preceding chapter how Jehovah's Witnesses reject almost every cardinal doctrine of the Christian faith, while at the same time staunchly maintaining that they are Christians. Since the Bible is admittedly the only criterion for determining who is and who is not a Christian, we shall briefly review some of the teachings of the Watch Tower. We shall then present the Biblical teachings relative to the several doctrines under consideration, and thereby determine exactly what is the true Scriptural evaluation of Jehovah's Witnesses' system of theology.

I. THE DEITY OF JESUS CHRIST

The deity of our Lord Jesus Christ is taught in many passages of Scripture, but we have for the sake of brevity selected texts which, in their respective contexts and in full accordance with the laws of hermeneutics and exegesis irrevocably teach the absolute deity of Jesus Christ as the eternally existent Word of God who became flesh (John 1:1, 14) for the redemption of lost mankind.

> 1. For unto us a child is born, unto us a son is given: and the government shall be upon his shoulder: and his name shall be called Wonderful, Counsellor, The mighty God, The everlasting Father, The Prince of Peace (Isaiah 9:6).

It may be seen from this quotation from Scripture that the child to be born and the son to be given possessed unusual titles for a child. Indeed, such titles have never been claimed in all the Hebrew Scriptures for anyone but Jehovah Himself, and were not Isaiah a major prophet, writing under the direction of the Holy Spirit — a fact which the Jews themselves confess — He would have been stoned to death under Moses' law (Blasphemy — Lev. 24:16) for daring to apply to an infant as yet unborn those titles which are by their very nature applicable only to Deity.

Isaiah therefore testifies in the true Messianic tradition that the child to be born was to be divine, i.e., "Wonderful, Counsellor, the Mighty God (El Gebor), the Everlasting Father (literally 'the Father of eternity,' Hebrew), the Prince of Peace." And this child, Matthew informs us, was Jesus Christ of Nazareth (Matt. 1:22, 23).

According to Isaiah 43:10, 11, Jehovah is the only God, He is elsewhere called "the mighty God" (Isa. 10:21), and the third chapter of Exodus, verse 6, identifies this same Being as "the God of Jacob" — proof positive to any student of Scripture and systematic theology that Jehovah and "the mighty God" are one and the Same (Jer. 32:18). Therefore, beyond dispute, both hermeneutically and exegetically,* Jesus Christ is Jehovah the Son "the Wonderful Counsellor, the mighty God, the everlasting Father, the Prince of Peace."

Jehovah's Witnesses object to the term "mighty God" as applied to Christ, pointing out that Christ is "a mighty god." And they claim that since there is no article in the Hebrew in Isaiah 9:6, therefore Jehovah God is not meant. However, as many scholars have pointed out, Isaiah 10:21 possesses no article either in the Hebrew, therefore using the same argument the God of Jacob is not Jehovah, a fact which would contradict Exodus 3:6, so despite the Witnesses' linguistics, the fact still remains that the Lord Jesus Christ is "the mighty God," article or no article being present, since His Deity is not contingent upon articular emphasis but upon the whole content of teaching throughout the Bible.

    2. In the beginning was the Word, and the Word was with God, and the Word was God (John 1:1)

* Comparison of texts and grammatical study.

I have dealt exhaustively with the problem of the translation of John1:1 in my book, *Jehovah of the Watch Tower,* so it is unnecessary at this time to go into great detail. But suffice it to say the translation which the Watch Tower employs, which would make John 1:1 read "a god"[1] instead of "God" is erroneous and unsupported by any good Greek scholarship, ancient or contemporary and is a translation rejected by all recognized scholars of the Greek language many of whom are not even Christians, and cannot fairly be said to be biased in favor of the orthodox contention.[2] Suffice it to say that John 1:1 teaches that Jesus Christ existed from all eternity, "the Word was God," "the Word was with God," ergo, the Word *is* God, a fact substantiated by the 14th verse of the same chapter, "The Word was made flesh, and dwelt among us (and we beheld his glory, the glory as of the only [one] begotten of the Father), full of grace and truth."[*]

The Gospel of John throughout its entirety teaches beyond reasonable doubt the absolute Deity of Jesus Christ and His unity of Nature with God the Father. John 1:1 is only the opening salvo, so to speak, of a great barrage of scriptural truth which levels to the intellectual rubble it is the scholastically shallow Christology of Jehovah's Witnesses.

> 3. Therefore the Jews sought the more to kill him, because he not only had broken the sabbath, but said also that God was his Father, making himself equal with God (John 5:18).

John 5:18 is clearly a narrative passage; that is, it is a record by the inspired writer of what he saw take place relative to the Lord Jesus Christ in this particular dispute

---

[1] See John 1:18 where no article appears in the Greek as in John 1:1 and yet the Witnesses render it "God" not "a god" grammatically inconsistent to the last!

[2] The Witnesses list a group of verses in the Appendix of their New World Translation which due to the lack of articular emphasis are supposed to "prove" the validity of their "a god" rendering. This linguistic dodge explodes, however, when Dr. Colwell's rule of Greek grammar is applied to John 1:1 and the selected texts the Witnesses have chosen. Colwell's Rule shows that a definite predicate nominative takes the article when it follows the verb; it does not do so when it precedes the verb as in John 1:1.

[*] See footnote 2 above.

with the Jews. John records that the Jews sought the more to kill Jesus because not only had He broken the Sabbath as they conceived of it, but He had called God His Father, which clearly in their thinking and in the thinking of John postulated equality with God or Deity. Jehovah's Witnesses have attempted to state during numerous interviews the author has had with their representatives, that John was merely *recording* what the Jews said, and therefore that the opinion that the Jews had does not *necessarily* mean that Christ claimed equality with God. The folly of this forced interpretation is the fact that it is John who states: "making himself equal with God." That is, it is John's impression not the Jews' which was recorded under the direct inspiration of the Holy Spirit, and even Jehovah's Witnesses who profess that the Bible is their sole rule of faith and practice would be loathe to say that what John recorded was not inspired by God!

We therefore see the Scriptures plainly teach in this context that Christ claimed equality with Jehovah, an equality based upon His eternal pre-existence and His true Nature, i.e., intrinsic Deity (Col. 2:9).

> 4. Jesus said unto them, Verily, verily, I say unto you, Before Abraham was, I am (John 8:58).

This verse of Scripture is perhaps the most damaging quotation in the entire book of John relative to Jehovah's Witnesses' opposition to the Deity of Christ. In one terse statement it decimates the entire fabricated Watch Tower theory that Jesus Christ, though existing before Abraham, was not One in substance with Jehovah of the Old Testament. To illustrate this point the New World Translation, which is a publication of the Watch Tower Bible and Tract Society (and a most faulty one at that in numerous places), *invents* a tense in the Greek and titles it "the perfect indefinite tense," a tense which does not exist in any known Greek grammar book, and renders John 8:58, "Before Abraham was I have been," thereby attempting to remove the present form of the verb "to be," i.e., "I am," which when cross-referenced with Exodus 3:14 clearly teaches that Jesus was claiming Jehovah-istic identity. This fact even the Jews understood as evidenced by the 59th verse where they picked up stones to kill Jesus under the Mosaic law which forbids any human being to claim the Nature of Deity (Lev. 24:16).

The Lord Jesus Christ, then, in the eighth chapter of John, obviously understood the Jews and by reprimanding them made the astounding claim that He had pre-existed from all eternity, thereby antedating Abraham and claiming for Himself Deity in unmistakable terms, "Before Abraham was, I am"; this is tantamount to saying, "Before Abraham existed I am Jehovah!"

> 5. And Thomas answered and said unto him, My Lord and my God (John 20:28).

Most all students of Scripture are familiar with so-called "doubting Thomas" who refused to believe that Jesus Christ had risen from the grave until he had thrust his finger into the wounds of Christ's hands and his hand into Christ's open side, a statement he later deeply regretted. John records for us in the 20th chapter how the Lord Jesus appeared after His resurrection in a physical form and then singling out Thomas offered His resurrection *body* as proof that He had truly vanquished the grave as a man and had risen in a bodily form. Thomas, it will be noted, wasted no time in doing what any human being would do when confronted with such divine evidence, he uttered the immortal phrase, "My Lord and my God," worshiping at the feet of his risen Saviour, and giving to Jesus Christ adoration and homage as "God manifest in the flesh." Now if Jehovah's Witnesses honestly want to be realistic, they will have to recognize two facts: First, Jesus appeared in physical form bearing the marks which He received upon the Cross — inescapable evidence that His was a bodily resurrection, not a spirit resurrection as they attempt to teach. Second, the Witnesses will also have to admit that under Mosaic law no one is entitled to worship but Jehovah

Himself (Exodus 20); therefore, when Thomas worshiped Jesus as "My Lord and my God" he was in effect committing blasphemy for which Christ would have immediately rebuked him, *unless* what Thomas was saying was true, namely, that Jesus was his Lord and his God, Jehovah, the Son. Since Jesus did not rebuke him, but instead continued on to teach His disciples more of His Identity and plans, the argument of the Watch Tower crumbles before this revelation of Scriptural truth. With Thomas then all true Christians can echo of the Lord Jesus Christ, "My Lord and my God."

> 6. For by him were all things created, that are in heaven, and that are in earth, visible and invisible, whether they be thrones, or dominions, or principalities, or powers: all things were created by him, and for him: And he is before all things, and by him all things consist (Colossians 1:16, 17).

The first chapter of Colossians is one of the truly great testimonies recorded in Scripture which prove that Jesus Christ is in the second Person of the Trinity or God the Son. In verses 16 and 17 the Apostle Paul portrays the Lord Jesus as the Creator of all things, whether they be visible or invisible, whether they be thrones or principalities or powers, Paul tells us all these things were created *for* Him and *by* Him. In addition to this Paul makes no small issue, in verse 17, of emphasizing the fact that Christ is *before* all things and that through Him all things consist, or literally "hold together." He is not therefore one of the "things," but their Creator — God.

> 7. Looking for that blessed hope, and the glorious appearing of the great God and our Saviour Jesus Christ (Titus 2:13).

With characteristic dogmatism Paul in his epistle to Titus declares that the Church is awaiting the "appearing of the glory of the great God and our Saviour Jesus Christ," who at His glorious second coming will raise the dead, transform the living Church to immortality and usher in the great and terrible day of judgment upon sin.

The Watch Tower Bible and Tract Society since it rejects the *visible* second coming of Christ and teaches instead an invisible "presence" of Christ, is most eager to circumvent the clear teaching of this text, which proves both the Deity of Jesus Christ and His physical second coming to judge the world.

The most conclusive bit of information in this text comes from a translation which the Watch Tower itself circulates, namely, the Emphatic Diaglott whose rendering of Titus 2:13 is as follows: "Waiting for the blessed hope, even the appearing of the glory of our great God and Saviour Jesus Christ."

Further comment is therefore deemed unnecessary at this time for in a translation circulated by the Watch Tower and recommended by them it is taught that Jesus Christ will *appear* — and such an appearance could only be visible if the Greek term means anything* — and further that He is "our great God and Saviour," a fact which the Watch Tower strenuously denies though one of their own publications strenuously affirms it!

We prefer to accept the rendering of the Emphatic Diaglott in this case because it happens to be grammatically correct and it most clearly proves the point which the historic Church has ever held, namely, that Jesus Christ is Lord of all, "our Great God and Saviour."

> 8. God, who at sundry times and in divers manners spake in times past unto the fathers by the prophets, Hath in these last days spoken unto us by his Son, whom he hath appointed heir of all things, by whom also he made the worlds: Who being the brightness of his glory, and the express image of his person, and upholding all things by the word of his power, when he had by himself purged our sins, sat down on the right hand of the Majesty on high (Hebrews 1:1-3).

Any thorough student of Scripture, reading the first four or five verses of the epistle to the Hebrews could come to no other conclusion than the fact that since Jesus Christ is called "the brightness of God's glory and the express image of His Person," therefore Christ Himself is *of* the Divine Nature. The Greek rendering of Hebrews 1:2 and 3 is extremely in-

---

* Greek — EPIPHANEIA used with PAROUSIA in II Thess. 2:8 for visible advent of Christ. See also II Tim. 1:10 where it is used for the first advent of Christ.

teresting, since it proves conclusively that the Lord Jesus Christ is the image of His Father and shares the very Nature of God. The Greek states, in fact, that Christ is "the effulgence of His glory and the image imprinted by His Nature or Substance." Christ is God's Character incarnate.

In a manner reminiscent of their Arian ancestors Jehovah's Witnesses deny vehemently that the Lord Jesus Christ possesses the Nature of Deity; in fact, they contend that He was created out of nothing, possessed an angelic nature, as Michael the Archangel before His incarnation, and further that during His sojourn on earth as a man He was a perfect man, no more, no less, or to quote the Watch Tower, "Certainly not the Supreme God Almighty in the flesh" (*Let God Be True,* edit. 1946, p. 87).

Perhaps more than any other book in the New Testament, the Epistle to the Hebrews proves beyond question the true Deity of Jesus Christ and teaches that not only is He our ascended High Priest and Intercessor before the Father, but that He is the Living Word of God (Hebrews 4:12), who judges the thoughts and intentions of our hearts and who remains the same "yesterday, today and forever." Jehovah's Witnesses strive constantly to reduce the Lord Jesus Christ in rank from the second person of the Triune Deity to a created being. However, let us keep in mind the writer of Hebrews admonition to the Church, namely, that our Saviour far from being a creature (regardless of the exalted rank one may assign to Him) is in truth and in deed the eternal Word of God, the radiance or effulgence of His Father's glory, the very image imprinted or impressed by the Nature of the Father — God manifest in the flesh, the fullness of the Godhead bodily (Heb. 1:1-3; I Tim. 3:16; Col. 2:9).*

> 9. I am Alpha and Omega, the beginning and the ending, saith the Lord, which is, and which was, and which is to come, the Almighty. I John, who also am your brother, and com-

* Note — That He was never Michael is proved by Jude 9 where Michael does not "dare" (Greek ETOLMESE) rebuke Satan. Jesus had no such inhibitions or restrictions (Matt. 4:10; Mark 8:33).

panion in tribulation, and in the kingdom and patience of Jesus Christ, was in the isle that is called Patmos, for the word of God, and for the testimony of Jesus Christ. . . . And he had in his right hand seven stars: and out of his mouth went a sharp twoedged sword: and his countenance was as the sun shineth in his strength. And when I saw him, I fell at his feet as dead. And he laid his right hand upon me, saying unto me, Fear not; I am the first and the last (Revelation 1: 8, 9, 16, 17).

These particular verses from the book of Revelation constitute one of the major pitfalls to the Christology of Jehovah's Witnesses. The reason for this is the fact that in Revelation 1:8 and 9 the Alpha and Omega is identified with Jehovah, whereas in verses 16 and 17 the Alpha and the Omega is specifically referred to as the Lord Jesus Christ. At the same time Jehovah is distinctly meant in the context as any linkage of the four verses together will quickly reveal to the interested student. Jehovah's Witnesses themselves translate Revelation 1:8 and 9 using the divine name Jehovah, whereas in Revelation 1:16 and 17 they are particularly silent when the *first* and the *last* (Alpha and Omega) is identified as the risen victorious Son of God — a blow indeed to their Arianism, a theology which would reduce the Son of God to the role of a created being.

In accordance with many passages of the Old Testament it cannot be denied by the Witnesses that Jehovah claims to be "the first and the last," and asserts Himself that besides Him "there is no other God" (Isa. 43:10).

We therefore see that if Jehovah Himself is the *first* and the *last* and the Alpha and Omega of Revelation 1:8 and 9, either there are *two* firsts and lasts (Rev. 1:16 and 17) or the texts are speaking of the *same* Being, i.e., the Triune God! Against such an argument, Jehovah's Witnesses have no defense, for Jesus Christ is clearly in these contexts revealed to be the *first* and the *last,* or Jehovah the Son, the second person of the Trinity, our coming King and their Judge.

The preceding examples from Scripture, which illustrate

the Deity of the Lord Jesus Christ, clearly reveal, we believe, what the entire tenure of Scripture teaching is; namely, that the eternal Word of God clothed Himself with humanity (John 1:1, 14) and dwelt among the sons of men, and through His sacrifice upon the Cross and His glorious triumph over death, as evidenced by the empty tomb, man might at last find peace with God, freedom from the penalty of sin, and power to please Him who is the only wise God, "the great God and our Saviour Jesus Christ" (Titus 2:13).

We shall conclude this section by briefly discussing the doctrine of the Trinity and citing some Scripture references.

II. THE DOCTRINE OF THE TRINITY

The doctrine of the Trinity is consistently abused by Jehovah's Witnesses in all their publications and public lectures as "pagan" and "a false un-Biblical doctrine" (*Make Sure of All Things*, p. 386). We cannot, of course, fully cover such a tremendous scope of knowledge as the Trinity embraces in the space allotted to us here, but we can make some pertinent observation which may clear the haze which exists in the minds of some people relative to the importance of this teaching.

Many times in the Old Testament (Gen. 1:26; Gen. 3:22; Gen. 11:7, etc.) *composite* unity is indicated within the Deity. While it is quite true that God cannot be conceived in corporeal terms, He has chosen to express Himself in a manner which would be meaningful to the minds of men. The fourth chapter of John's gospel, verse 24, indicates the true Nature of God is pure Spirit, and other portions of the Scripture, (John 1:1, 8:58, Hebrews 1:2, 3, etc.) unmistakably point out that Jesus Christ shares this spiritual Nature, the independent exercise of which He voluntarily surrendered at His incarnation (John 1:14, Phil. 2:8), so that He might truly be one of the sons of men. We ought never to forget in our study of the Trinity that God is Triune, *not* triplex. His nature is not a mathematical contradiction, it is merely outside the realm of mathematical application (not

1+1+1=3 or 1+1+1=1 but 1×1×1=1). The Trinity itself is a mystery or "a holy secret." It is incomprehensible. It can never be fully understood. The best we have in Scripture is the declaration that God is one Nature manifested in three Persons, the Father, the Son and Holy Spirit, in whose name Christ commanded us to baptize and in whose name we are to make disciples of all nations.

In the third chapter of Matthew's gospel, verses 16 and 17, Matthew records the baptism of the Lord Jesus Christ, at which time the Father spoke from Heaven, the Son was baptized and present upon the earth, and the Holy Spirit descended in the form of a dove — strong evidence, indeed, of the threefold unity which exists within the Godhead. The beloved disciple, John, tells us in the fifth chapter of his gospel, verse 23, "All men should honor the Son *even* as they honor the Father," a fact Jehovah's Witnesses should take cognizance of in no uncertain terms, since all of their professed love and obedience for Jehovah amounts to nothing in the light of John's words; for while professing to honor the Father they have indeed dishonored His Son, whom God has commanded that all men should honor *even* as they honor Him.

Far from being destitute for verses to support the doctrine of the Trinity, Christians can indeed turn to not a few places in Scripture which indicate definite plurality and interrelationship between the members of the Godhead. Two such cardinal examples are found in the 14th chapter of St. John's gospel, verses 16 and 26. In verse 16 Christ said, "And *I* will pray the *Father*, and he shall give you another Comforter, that he may abide with you for ever." It should be noted that Christ states that *He* will pray, that the prayer will be directed to the *Father* and that the Father would give another *Comforter*, i.e., the Holy Spirit — proof that there is more to the doctrine of the Trinity than Jehovah's Witnesses would like to have their followers believe!

Verse 26 of this same chapter, "But the Comforter, which

is the *Holy Ghost,* whom *the Father* will send in my name, he shall teach you all things, and bring all things to your remembrance, whatsoever *I* have said unto you" again demonstrates the unity of the Godhead, all three Persons being mentioned in the same verse and declared to be in unity as to the workings of Deity. See also Luke 1:35 where the Trinity is seen.

Much more could be said about the doctrine of the Trinity, but space does not allow us to go into an extended discussion at this time. For those interested in a thorough coverage of this subject, *Jehovah of the Watch Tower,* chapters 3 and 8 cover the subject quite adequately and still remain unanswered by Jehovah's Witnesses or their official organs, the Watch Tower and Awake.

III. The Resurrection of Jesus Christ

As we have seen in Chapter III, the Watch Tower Bible and Tract Society has as one of the cardinal planks in its doctrinal platform a teaching completely alien to historic biblical Christianity, the dogma that Jesus Christ was raised from the grave a spirit.

In words that no one could possibly misinterpret the Watch Tower denies the physical resurrection of the Lord Jesus Christ, stating that ". . . the King Christ Jesus was put to death in the flesh and was resurrected in an invisible spirit creature" (*Let God Be True,* edit. 1946, p. 122). Following up this clear-cut statement on page 272 of the same edition the Watch Tower stated, "This first-born one from the dead was not raised out of the grave a human creature, but he was raised a spirit." Thus there can be no doubt as to the true nature of this Watch Tower dogma.

It would be possible to refer to many verses of Scripture which directly contradict this Watch Tower teaching. However, there are three excellent examples furnished in the gospels of Luke and John, respectively, to which we shall now refer briefly.

In the 24th chapter of Luke's Gospel, beginning at verse

13 and going through verse 49, the risen Christ is represented as appearing to two of His disciples traveling on
the road to Emmaus. In verse 16 the Scripture clearly states
"that their eyes were *holden* (Greek — "held from recogniz-
ing Him" — Robertson) that they should not know him." This
is a clear indication indeed that although it was the risen
Lord Jesus Christ, nevertheless by an act of His will He
veiled their eyes so that they could not recognize Him. Thus
it was possible for Him to speak with His disciples, and at the
same time for them to be totally ignorant of His true Identity.
As the chapter continues Christ reveals Himself through the
conversation which He has taken charge of and is leading to its
supernatural conclusion. In verse 31 the full radiance of His
resurrection glory shines through to them, "And their eyes were
opened and they knew him; and he vanished out of their sight."
Then and only then did they come to the full realization that
the "stranger" with whom they walked and talked was indeed
the Risen Lord of Glory.

Reading on through the chapter, we notice these same
disciples returned to Jerusalem and told the eleven who
were gathered together (doubtless in prayer and medita-
tion) that they had seen the risen Lord, and even as they
spoke "Jesus himself stood in the midst of them, and saith
unto them, Peace be unto you."

The reaction of the disciples to the presence of their
risen Master is magnificently captured by Luke, who states,
". . . they were terrified and affrighted, and supposed that
they had seen a spirit." This is extremely important in
view of the fact that Jehovah's Witnesses teach that Christ
came out of the grave a spirit, and if the text had ended
with verse 37, they would have strong ground to stand
upon — at least in this instance. But as we shall see, the text
continues on. What the disciples assumed to be an apparition
or a spirit suddenly dispels all their doubts as to His true
Nature and Identity, for our risen Lord said, "Why are ye

troubled? and why do thoughts arise in your hearts? Behold my hands and my feet, that it is I myself: handle me, and see; for a spirit hath *not* flesh and bones, as ye see me have. And when he had thus spoken, he shewed them his hands and his feet" (verses 38-40).

No honest person, reading the former quotations from the Watch Tower's own publications, and then reading verses 36 through 43, could possibly come to any conclusion other than the fact that Jesus Christ was resurrected bodily from the dead, and that by His own words He defined the nature of a spirit, stating that it did not have flesh and bones "as ye see me have!" Further than this as incontestable evidence, "He showed them his hands and his feet."

To further establish the fact that His was a bodily resurrection, in verse 42 Christ partook of a piece of broiled fish and of a honeycomb. The Scripture says (verse 43), "And he took it, and did eat before them." This is hardly the behavior one would expect from the "spirit-creature" of Jehovah's Witnesses theological myth; in fact, this Being by His very Nature and presence destroyed the entire Russellite teaching of a spirit resurrection and established beyond question the fact that Christ came forth from the tomb in an immortal form, truly God and truly man, whose physical image we shall one day bear when this corruption puts on incorruption and this mortal puts on immortality (I Cor. 15).

The second irrefutable biblical evidence for the physical resurrection of our Lord is found in the 20th chapter of John's gospel where it is a very simple matter to note that the disciple Thomas doubted the literal, bodily resurrection of our Lord; in fact, Thomas went so far as to say, "Except I shall see in his hands the print of the nails, and put my finger into the print of the nails, and thrust my hand into his side, I will not believe" (John 20:25).

Reading on through the chapter, verses 26 through 31, the context reveals that eight days from His first appearance to His disciples, "came Jesus, the doors being shut, and stood in the midst, and said, Peace be unto you. Then saith he to Thomas, Reach hither thy finger, and behold my hands; and reach hither thy hand, and thrust it into my side: and be not faithless, but believing" (John 20:26, 27).

Now one thing is most evident from this account of Christ's appearance to the disciples, Thomas being present, and that is the certainty of the physical appearance of Jesus Christ. Jesus, if He were the "spirit-creature" of Russellite mythology and Jehovah's Witnesses theology would never have invited Thomas to stretch forth his finger to behold His hand, or to reach his hand into His very side, *unless* there were physical hands that Thomas could touch and a physical side into which Thomas could have thrust his hand. This is the only logical conclusion from both the language and the context of this chapter.

The third and final proof of Christ's bodily resurrection comes from the mouth of our Lord Himself who prophesied the nature of His conquest over death by stating to the antagonistic Jews, "Destroy this temple and in three days I will raise it up" (John 2:17-19). John tells us that "he spake of the temple of his body" (v. 21); certainly *not* His Spirit as Jehovah's Witnesses try to teach. Thus from the final authority, Christ Himself, His bodily resurrection is taught.

We may see from these prime examples (Luke 24, John 2 and John 20) that the resurrection of Jesus Christ was indeed a physical resurrection, and although our Lord possessed what Paul describes in I Corinthians 15 as a "spiritual" body, the text does not state that it is a "spirit," and in the Greek there is a great difference between the two. A spiritual body is a physical form possessing spiritual characteristics, whereas a spirit is merely the manifestation of *spiritual* substance (i.e., angels, demons, etc.; see I Sam. 28:14ff. where Samuel appears as a spirit, his body having not yet been resurrected).

The resurrection of the Lord Jesus Christ, far from being illusory or phantom-like, was indeed the direct fulfillment of

God's promise to raise His Holy One bodily from the dead and not to allow Him to see corruption. Thus Christ Jesus emerged from the valley of death an immortal man, forever exempt from decay or death, possessing a form which we some day by His grace shall likewise possess when He shall come for His Church (I Thess. 4; I Cor. 15).

Jehovah's Witnesses, by promulgating their "spirit resurrection" theory, are found to be in direct contradiction to the teaching of Scripture and all who would worship God in spirit and in truth are urged to shun their unscriptural position which is indeed a danger for the unwary and "a way that seemeth right unto a man, but the end thereof are the ways of death."

We have seen in this chapter, relative to three of the cardinal doctrines of the Christian faith, i.e., the doctrine of the Deity of Christ, the Trinity of God and the physical resurrection of Christ, how Jehovah's Witnesses are in direct variance with the teachings of the Bible. If space were available we might carry out a searching survey of all their cardinal doctrines, comparing them with Scripture, knowing that they are in almost every instance contradictory to the basic principles of the Gospel of Jesus Christ. For those interested in a more detailed analysis of this problem, my book, *Jehovah of the Watch Tower*, a 230-page volume, exhaustively covers the history and doctrines of the Watch Tower and contains a refutation of the whole system. To aid the interested reader the following reference verses are supplied relative to principal doctrines of the Christian faith, references which directly contradict the teachings of the Watch Tower on the specific doctrines in question:

REFERENCES

1. The Trinity: John 1:1, Genesis 1:26, 11:7, Isaiah 9:6, Matthew 28:19, John 14:16, 26.
2. The Deity of Christ: John 1:1, 14, 18, 5:18, 8:58, 20:28, 17:1-5, Phil. 2:8-11, Col. 2:9, Heb. 1:1-4.

3. The Atonement: John 1:29, Rev. 13:8, Lev. 17:11, Heb. 9:22, I Peter 2:24, Col. 1:20, II Cor. 5:15.
4. The Return of Christ (Visible): Matt. 24:30, Rev. 1:7, I Thess. 4:16,17, Zech. 12:10.
5. The Resurrection of Christ (Physical): John 2:17-19, 20:27, 28, Luke 24:39-44, Mark 16:14, I Cor. 15:15.
6. Human Government: Rom. 13:1-7.
7. The Existence of Hell and Eternal Punishment: Matt. 5:22, 8:11, 12, 13:42-50, 25:41, 46, II Peter 2:17, Jude 13.
8. Satan the Devil: Matt. 25:41, Rev. 20:10.
9. The Existence of the Soul as a Conscious Entity: Gen. 1:26, 5:1, I Cor. 11:7, Job 32:8, Acts 7:59, II Cor. 4:12, 13.
10. The Kingdom of Heaven: Luke 17:20-26, Rev. 22: 1-5, 14.

CHAPTER FIVE

THE WATCH TOWER AND BLOOD TRANSFUSION[1]

In recent months, various newspapers and periodicals have mentioned in no small proportions the peculiar views of Jehovah's Witnesses in regard to transfusions of human blood. Since the Witnesses masquerade as "a sect of Fundamentalists" and call themselves Christians, it behooves those of us who do represent orthodox Christianity to set the record straight. Recently the authors (Martin and Klann) spent considerable time in research on the Witnesses' latest doctrine of blood transfusion. We visited the Watch Tower publication plant in Brooklyn, interviewed various Witnesses on their transfusion dogma, and collected all of their writings available on the subject. We, therefore, write this chapter fully understanding the Witnesses' views and from first-hand knowledge, not hearsay.

Following the death of Judge J. F. Rutherford (official voice of the Watch Tower Theocratic Organization), in January, 1942, a new doctrine began to develop under the succeeding regime headed by Nathan Homer Knorr. The Judge, like the "Pastor" (who died October 31, 1916), gradually faded into the Russellite shadows, and a new teaching foreign even to the Judge's prolific pen crept into the Theocratic fold. By some method of reasoning not connected with the processes of logical

[1] The following chapter appears in the book, *Jehovah of the Watch Tower,* and is included in this booklet in answer to the many requests for its separate publication, independent of the volume in which it appears.

thought, the Watch Tower suddenly "discovered" that blood transfusions were Biblically forbidden! Unhampered by the fact that the Bible never speaks on the subject (for it was completely unknown in that era), *The Watch Tower* announced (July 1, 1945), in an article entitled, "Sanctity of Blood," that it was a violation of Jehovah's covenant to transfuse human blood, even if the life of the patient was at stake. This new "revelation" of the Russellite prophets caused no end of protest from informed medical men who knew that human life was in jeopardy and that they were sworn to preserve it. Of course, we would agree with Jehovah's Witnesses on the issue involved if it were based on Scriptural grounds, but in no sense can their arguments be supported from the Bible. Russellite thought on the subject seems to be revealed in their odd interpretation of the Levitical priesthood rulings on the office of sacrificial blood. Let us then prayerfully consider and weigh the entire teaching of the Bible on this matter, not just isolated verses the Witnesses have seized upon because they suit their temporary need for a new propaganda weapon.

In *Awake* magazine, May 22, 1951, page 3, Jehovah's Witnesses quote Genesis 9:4, Leviticus 3:17, 7:27, and 17: 10, 11, 14, and maintain that these texts support their refusal to recognize human blood transfusions. We shall now examine these references and see if their contentions are textually valid.

"Flesh with the life thereof, which is the blood thereof, shall ye not eat" (Gen. 9:4, as quoted in *Awake*). This verse as it appears in context has not the remotest connection with human blood, much less transfusions. In the previous verse of the same chapter, Jehovah clearly tells Noah that He is speaking in reference to animals and *their* flesh and blood. God told Noah that animal flesh was for food with but one provision — that he *eat not of the blood*. "Every moving thing that liveth shall be meat for you; even as the green herb have I given you all things. But flesh with the life thereof, which is the blood thereof, *shall ye not eat*" (Gen. 9:3, 4, A.V.).

Jehovah's Witnesses go on further in their article ("Children — Do They Belong to Parents or to the State?") to declare that Leviticus 3:17 and 7:27 forbid blood transfusions. Once again, the text-lifting Russellites disregard the meaning of the Levitical ordinance pertaining to sacrifices and burnt offerings.

"It shall be a perpetual statute for your generations throughout all your dwellings, that ye *eat* neither fat nor blood" (Lev. 3:17, A.V.).

"Whatsoever soul it be that *eateth* any manner of blood, even that soul shall be cut off from his people" (Lev. 7:27, A.V.).

To the well oriented Bible student little need be said for these two verses in the way of a thorough explanation. The third chapter of Leviticus clearly speaks of sacrifices and offerings *to be eaten as food*, and speaks of animal blood being *eaten*, *not* human blood being transfused! Leviticus 7:27 again refers to animal blood as food eaten and digested with no possible reference to transfusion. Rounding out their expedition into the Old Testament in vain hopes of re-tooling their tiresome propaganda machine, Jehovah's Witnesses set upon the seventeenth chapter of Leviticus as an argument against blood transfusions. In keeping with their habitual trait of conveniently overlooking damaging Scriptural evidence, the Witnesses fail to mention the context of the verses they quote. *Awake*[2] lists the references as Leviticus 17:10, 11, 14, but strangely omits verses 12 and 13 which clarify the texts. Verse 13 reads: "And whatsoever man there be of the children of Israel, or of the strangers that sojourn among you, which hunteth and catcheth any *beast or fowl* that may be *eaten*; he shall even pour out the blood thereof, and cover it with dust."

[2] The second largest Watch Tower publication.

This text clearly shows, as does the entire context of the chapter, that it refers *primarily* to animal's blood and eating, since cannibalism was expressly forbidden under the commandment, "Thou shalt not murder," as well as in other teachings of the Scripture (Ex. 20). As a matter of interest, it might also be noted that whenever human sacrifice is mentioned in the Bible, it is always declared abominable to the Lord. Israel was expressly forbidden to kill, much less eat one another under penalty of immediate judgment, as it is written, "Whoso sheddeth man's blood by man shall his blood be shed: for in the image of God made he man" (Gen. 9:6).

Jehovah's Witnesses cite many more passages against the eating of blood from the Old Testament. In the New Testament they continue in the same vein. The writer of the article in *Awake* lists Acts 15:19, 20, 28, 29, and 21:15, to corroborate the Old Testament teaching on the eating of blood from the New Covenant. But now let us look at what the Witnesses are trying to prove and see if the point is valid.

First of all, orthodox Christianity recognizes and observes the rulings on the *eating* of blood as found in the Old and New Testaments. However, we cannot agree with the conclusion drawn by Jehovah's Witnesses. The Watch Tower insists that the transfusion of human blood through the veins is as much feeding the body as eating through the mouth. This is indeed a clever deduction, but in view of the Scripture's true teaching it cannot stand up.

In the Old Testament Jehovah forbad eating the blood of animals as unclean, and likewise the blood of man. Blood transfusion is in the technical medical sense a "feeding" of the body when disease or anemia lower the blood count and "starve" the vital organs. It does not involve in any possible sense (1) the sacrifice of life, (2) the impairment of another's health, or (3) the violation of a code of sacrificial laws as found in the Old Testament. Jehovah's Witnesses cannot produce one single verse of Scripture in reference to the blood of man, either in transfusion or ceremonial sacrifice, which in any way could be construed as an argument against saving another's life. When one gives a transfusion, it is not a sacrifice of life, and the *eating* of forbidden blood, but a *transference of life* from one person to another, a gift of strength offered in the spirit of mercy and charity. Anyone who has beheld another dying for lack of blood and has witnessed the disintegration of human life can appreciate the great good blood transfusions have accomplished on the whole. Of course, there are cases where infection or even death occur, but the percentage is small proportionately and does not warrant comparison. Nevertheless, Jehovah's Witnesses persist with ever heightening waves of propaganda to condemn all who sanction or participate in blood transfusions. Say the Witnesses, "So, whether one eats congealed blood in unbled meat, or drinks it at a slaughterhouse, or takes it by intravenous feeding at a hospital, it is still a violation of divine restriction that forbids taking blood into the system" (see *Awake*, May 22, 1951, page 4).

This is only one of the many dogmatic assertions by the Witnesses that they are *the* authority on Jehovah's Word, the Bible. Despite the fact that they will not in scholastic debate answer criticism on this point and many others in biblical theology, they persist in playing *the* fountain of truth and "Jehovah's Theocratic Organization."

"Jesus poured His (Blood) out as a ransom price, not as a transfusion" (*Awake*, page 6), the Watch Tower declares, and attempts to argue all opposition to silence with myriads of tracts, pamphlets and books.

The confused Russellite Watch Tower has fought blood transfusion even to the high courts of our land. In 1951[3] (October 31), young Jonathan Sheton was taken from his mother Hazel, a confirmed Jehovah's Witness who was willing to offer up the life of her child who was suffering

[3] *Awake*, January 22, 1952, p. 160.

from a ruptured appendix, rather than submit him to blood transfusion. This unfortunate woman did not take her position because the Bible taught it, but because the Watch Tower Bible and Tract Society *said* the Bible taught it. This is a far different matter indeed!

On April 17, 1951,[4] Mrs. Rhoda Labrenz of Chicago, another ardent Jehovah's Witness, refused her needy daughter, Cheryl Lynn, a blood transfusion on the grounds that "...We can't break Jehovah's law." It is indeed a sad turn of events when a mother will abandon her child to possible death simply because the Watch Tower of Jehovah's Witnesses *says this is* Jehovah's Law![5] A recent case similar to this one, but one with bitter and tragic results, was recorded thusly by the *New York Daily News.*

> A young father and mother said today they followed "God's will" in refusing a blood transfusion on religious grounds while their 9-day-old baby died.
>
> A doctor stood by, anxiously hoping the parents would change their minds. Authorities also sought to take the baby away from the parents by court order. But they were too late.
>
> The father, Thomas Grzyb, 20, said: "It was God's will. I would not have the child come back to life if it was against God's will. If I am called a murderer, that is God's will.
>
> "We want more children. But if such a thing happens again and the child dies, that will be God's way too." Grzyb said, "I will not interfere with God's will."
>
> His wife, Barbara, 18, sobbed, "My baby, my baby," over and over. But she agreed with her husband. Both are members of Jehovah's Witnesses and said they followed Biblical teachings that blood must not be used as food.

One more example of the stubborn resistance bordering on fanaticism which Jehovah's Witnesses display on the issue of blood transfusion is found in the *New York Daily News*

[4] *Chicago Herald American,* April 18, 1951.

[5] Proof that the Witnesses follow the Watch Tower's edicts and interpretations of the Bible is found in the fact that no Jehovah's Witnesses objected to blood transfusions *until* the Watch Tower pronounced on the subject. So the claim of the Witnesses that they are only obeying Scripture evaporates in the light of facts.

of April 27, 1952. We quote the news item here in its entirety.

ARREST "WITNESSES," GIVE WOMAN BLOOD

Odessa, Tex., April 27 (U.P.) — The father and two brothers of a critically injured woman were arrested today when they tried to prevent a doctor from giving her a blood transfusion considered necessary to save her life.

Marie Oliff, 20, was given the blood as the three men were removed from the hospital room where she had lain unconscious for a week.

The girl suffered a compound skull fracture, a fractured pelvis and fractures of both legs in an automobile collision, and her physician said she might die if she did not receive a transfusion immediately.

Her father and brothers had stood guard at her room and said they would resort to force if anyone tried to give her blood. Members of the Jehovah's Witnesses religious sect, they claimed the Bible forbids transfusions.

Miss Oliff regained consciousness briefly today and physicians decided to ask her if she would overrule her family.

First they asked if she was a member of Jehovah's Witnesses. "No," she replied.

"Do you want a transfusion, if one is necessary?" a doctor asked.

"Yes," she said.

Her brothers, John, 27, and Ben, 23, of 124 Columbia Heights, Brooklyn, were in the room.

"Tell them you're a member of the Jehovah's Witnesses and you don't want a blood transfusion," John told his sister several times.

Her father, William Oliff, 54, a Midland, Tex., trailer camp operator, told doctors: "You're trying to kill my girl."

Acting under a court order, the doctors called police, who ousted the three men from the hospital room.

"You can't treat us like this unless you arrest us," John said.

"All right," an officer replied, "All three of you are under arrest. You're charged with disturbing peace. Let's go to jail."

The three were arraigned before Justice of the Peace Jack Parker and held in $250 bond each.

Miss Oliff's divorced husband, Clyde Wright of Odessa, got an injunction Wednesday restraining the family from interfering with a transfusion.

Think soberly on this brief story for one moment if you will, and the horror of this new Watch Tower dogma cannot help but grip you. Here were a father and two brothers so devoted to what the Watch Tower *says* the Bible teaches, that they were willing to sacrifice the life of their own flesh and blood on the Russellite altar of ignorance. Even Judge Rutherford with all his faults would shudder at this travesty upon reason and Scripture.

A final example of Russellite blindness, all too common among Jehovah's Witnesses, is found in a recent case here reproduced from the *New York Mirror* of June 20, 1955.

Religious convictions bowed to an emergency court order Sunday and a frail, nine-day-old girl was rushed to an Englewood, N. J., hospital for a blood transfusion against which her parents had fought as "contrary to the law of God."

An emergency midnight court session, held in Palisades Police headquarters, ended in the issuance of an order placing Gail Bertinato in the custody of Bergen County's Welfare Department after three physicians warned that unless the transfusions were given quickly she would die.

Her parents, Louis, 26, and Gloria, 24, of 336 Second St., Palisades Park, who had fought since Friday to prevent the transfusion, took their defeat without rancor and told newsmen: "Our objections are scriptural. We were only doing our Christian duty. We had no other choice. God's law is supreme over any man made law; you just don't break the law of God."

Members of Jehovah's Witnesses, they told the court that they believe blood transfusions are against the teachings of the Bible.

Gail, born June 10 in Jersey City, fell ill Friday and was found to be suffering from an RH negative factor, which means that her red corpuscles are not produced rapidly enough to meet the body's needs. Dr. C. T. Markert of Ridgefield Park told the parents that their baby was critically ill and should have an immediate transfusion.

But the parents balked. Markert notified police Chief Leonard Cottrell, who conferred with Bergen County Prosecutor Guy W. Calissi. Digging into his law books, Calissi came up with a little-known statute under which children may be placed in the county's custody in emergency cases.

He filed a complaint with Juvenile and Domestic Relations Court Judge Martin J. Kole late Saturday night — and Kole, ordering an immediate hearing issued a show-cause order requiring the parents to appear before him.

Cottrell drove to their home to make one more effort to persuade them to consent to the transfusion. When they refused, he took them before Kole — and it was then that the three doctors voiced an unanimous warning that without a transfusion Gail could not live.

Rushed to the hospital by Cottrell and juvenile authorities as soon as the hearing was over, Gail was given an emergency transfusion at 2 a.m. Hospital spokesmen described the baby's condition later as "still critical, but showing improvement."

Her parents said they will visit her "as often as the doctor permits us."

In spite of such developments as the *Mirror* reported, Jehovah's Witnesses continue their blissful ploddings on ground that even angels fear to tread, and play with the lives of little children who are helpless to protect themselves. *The Watch Tower* further declares, on page 415 (July 1, 1951), "Blood transfusions are *not* Christlike . . . and doing it in disobedience to God's commands could cost one eternal life."[6]

Following hard upon the heels of the fleeing "Religionists," of whom the late lamented Judge J. F. Rutherford once said, "They shall go down in defeat biting the dust as they go,"[7] the zealous Witnesses affirm that "transfusions are a violation of the everlasting covenant."[8] Just which covenant they are referring to remains a mystery since the Bible speaks of no covenant even remotely connected with blood transfusions. The American Red Cross disclosed the following figures on the marvelous life-saving accomplishment of blood donations

---

[6] It was the Lord Jesus who said: "Whosoever shall offend one of these little ones that believe in me, it is better for him that a millstone were hanged about his neck, and he were cast into the sea" (Mark 9:42). The Witnesses would therefore do well to remember these words when they tamper with the lives of innocent children.

[7] Radio address, "Children of the King," Record (7) by J. F. Rutherford.

[8] *Awake*, February 22, 1951.

in a booklet entitled, "Blood, Your Gift of Life." We quote portions of the article to emphasize the tremendous good blood transfusions have accomplished.

BLOOD IN WORLD WAR II

On February 4, 1941, a miracle of blood donations began. At Army and Navy request, the American National Red Cross then started a blood donor service, to get plasma for the U. S. Armed Forces.

It was a joint project of the Red Cross and the National Research Council. The Red Cross set up, staffed, and operated blood procurement centers, recruited the donors, and paid the major costs of obtaining the blood. The National Research Council, which already had set up a Sub-committee on Blood Substitutes, directed all the technical phases under a panel of top-notch blood experts.

One figure sums up the dramatic story — 13,326,242 pints of blood given freely by the American people before the program ended on September 15, 1945. At the peak, they gave a pint of blood every two seconds. In one week, after the invasion of Normandy, Americans gave 123,284 pints, and contributed more than 5,300,000 pints in 1944 alone . . .

Giving blood is simple and painless. The average donor gave blood twice, about 1,500,000 gave three times, and 150,000 gave a gallon (eight pints) apiece. There were even 3,000 persons who gave two gallons or more. The givers all were 18 to 60 years old, men and women, of all races and creeds.

Plasma went abroad by ship and plane, and moved up with the troops. The donors knew what good it was doing, even before a Navy captain, giving a laconic report on the invasion of Tarawa. said: "6,000 pints of plasma went ashore with the Marines; 4,000 came back in the veins of wounded Marines . . ."

By August, 1944, whole blood was being flown to Europe, and by November, it was winging to the Pacific. Only group O blood — the universal type — was used.

Blood helped immeasurably to write a brilliant wartime medical record — the survival of more than 95 per cent of all wounded American servicemen . . .

To meet these needs, one of the greatest health steps in history was started in 1948 — the National Blood Program of the American Red Cross. It was founded on the firm belief that Americans would give blood to aid fellow citizens in peace, as they did for fighting men in war. Its success in three years has justified that faith . . .

By the end of 1950, 1,064,000 individuals had given 1,400,000 pints of blood to their fellowmen, as a free gift, and this year the rate of donations is spiraling upward. The blood and plasma and blood fractions went to 2,300 hospitals, to 134 independent clinics, and to 550 physicians who needed the supply in their own offices.

There then were 1,158 Red Cross chapters participating in 891 counties, with the blood program serving hospitals in areas containing 50,000,000 population.

Bloodmobiles range out from the centers to collect blood from people in smaller communities, and to deliver blood to people in need in those communities . . .

The benefits from this voluntary giving of blood have been immeasurable. Blood from the blood program has saved lives on operating tables, on highways, in train wrecks, in all manner of emergencies. The gift of blood has permitted operations that could not otherwise have been attempted, or supplied blood to aid surgical patients. It is not unusual these days for one person to receive eight or ten pints of blood before, during, and after a serious operation.

As one illustration of the value: Mothers often hemorrhage during childbirth, and need blood. *Immediate availability* of the blood can mean life, instead of death. In Rochester, New York, after a regional center was established, death rates from childbirth hemorrhages were cut to 1/10th what they had been eighteen months earlier.

These are only a few of the verifiable facts about the gigantic life-saving accomplishments of blood transfusions. Jehovah's Witnesses can offer but pitiful unscriptural criticism of so great a life-saving charity. The Lord Jesus said, "Greater love hath no man than this, that a man lay down his life for his friends" (John 15:13 A.V.). It must be plain to any rational person who studies the Scriptures without the Watch Tower's interpretations, that Christ understood suffering in others and healed its causes whenever He encountered it. How much more should those of us His servants be ever ready to alleviate the pain and suffering of others if it is not contrary to the clear pronouncements of Scripture and if it lies within our power. The Bible never speaks against transfusion in any form, only against "eating blood" in a purely dietary — sacrificial manner.

CHAPTER SIX

THE FAITH ONCE DELIVERED UNTO THE SAINTS

Throughout the whole panorama of Scripture the Holy Spirit has spoken to the Church of Jesus Christ regarding the doctrinal darkness which would toward the end of the ages engulf the world with such cleverness and power that it would deceive if possible even the elect. Beginning with the Lord Jesus in Matthew 7, verses 15 and 16, "Beware of false prophets . . ." the Spirit of God sounds a warning note to the heart of every Christian which should find a sympathetic hearing. It was no less an authority than the Apostle Paul who repeatedly gave vent to his convictions that "grievous wolves" (Acts 20:29-31) would infiltrate the Church of Christ, that they would "deceive" (Eph. 4:14), and that they would be "enemies of the Cross of Christ" (Phil. 3:18), possessing a "form of godliness, but denying the power thereof" (II Tim. 3:1-5, 7, 9, 13).

These individuals Peter further described as "false teachers among you, who privily (secretly) shall bring in damnable heresies" (II Pet. 2:1-6, 12, 17), and that they would by their very nature and teaching "deny the Lord that bought them."

Added to the voices of Peter and Paul are the testimonies of John and Jude, "many false prophets are gone out into the world" (I John 4:1), individuals who deny "the Lord God, and our Lord, Jesus Christ" (Jude 4, 12, 13) and who will have great success in leading many down the corridors of eternal death.

With these warnings so clearly given Christians today

61

can have no excuse for not heeding the commands of Scripture. For not only are we to preach the Gospel of Christ ("preach the Word") but we are, in the words of Jude, to "earnestly contend for the faith which was once delivered unto the saints" (Jude 3). We are engaged today in spiritual warfare against "another jesus," a "different spirit" and "another gospel" (II Cor. 11:3, 4), a being who is masqueraded to the world by "the god of this world" as the answer to the spiritual and temporal problems of mankind. It is against this "jesus" that Paul warns us. It is against this spirit that we are to strive. It is against his gospel that we are to preach "the truth as it is in Jesus." Paul tells us in II Timothy 4:1-5 that we are not only to preach the Word, but that we are to reprove, to rebuke, and to exhort with all longsuffering and doctrine. For the time will come when men will not endure sound doctrine but "will gather to themselves teachers who will tickle their ears and the truth of God will be turned into fables." The Church today ignores these warnings at her peril and at the peril of millions of souls who are sucked each year into the raging maw of cult doctrines. It is a known fact that all the major cults deny the great foundational doctrines of the Gospel: The Trinity, the Deity of Christ, the vicarious atonement, and the physical resurrection, by either changing the terminology to suit their own means, or by denying outright these great cardinal truths.

Jehovah's Witnesses are just one of the cults who practice these deceptive activities, and it is well that Christians and non-Christians alike be alerted to their methods "whereby they lie in wait to deceive" (Eph. 4:14).

The answer to Jehovah's Witnesses can only be found by coming to the realization that error can only be counteracted by sound doctrinal knowledge and training. Until pastors, teachers, and those whose responsibility it is to train Christian leaders come to the full realization that cultism today is surging forward as never before in our history, and that the Church is presently unequal to her task, we shall continue to fight a losing battle against the rising tides of cultism.

The Watch Tower capitalizes upon ignorance and confusion, and while it is true that its emissaries do not know too much about the great doctrines of Scripture, they know enough to confuse and confound the average Christian who quite often knows *what* he believes but more than likely does not know *why* he believes it!

In the sixth chapter of his Epistle to the Ephesians the great Apostle Paul counsels faithful Christians to prepare themselves, or more literally to arm themselves, for the battle in the heavenlies against the "methods of the devil." Let us listen to His Word:

Finally, my brethren, be strong in the Lord, and in the power of his might. Put on the whole armour of God, that ye may be able to stand against the wiles of the devil. For we wrestle not against flesh and blood, but against principalities, against powers, against the rulers of the darkness of this world, against spiritual wickedness in high places. Wherefore take unto you the whole armour of God, that ye may be able to withstand in the evil day, and having done all, to stand. Stand therefore, having your loins girt about with truth, and having on the breastplate of righteousness; And your feet shod with the preparation of the gospel of peace; Above all, taking the shield of faith, wherewith ye shall be able to quench all the fiery darts of the wicked. And take the helmet of salvation, and the sword of the Spirit, which is the word of God: Praying always with all prayer and supplication in the Spirit, and watching thereunto with all perseverance and supplication for all saints; And for me, that utterance may be given unto me, that I may open my mouth boldly, to make known the mystery of the gospel (Eph. 6:10-19).

Further comment on the situation here described is unnecessary, except to state that it is counsel we cannot afford to ignore any longer. Let us therefore heed the divine warnings of Scripture. Let us prepare ourselves against the deceptive activities of the "other jesus," his "different spirit," and "another gospel," and arm ourselves as God has commanded us with His whole armour, for then and then only will we be able to stand against the methods and devices of the devil who opposes vigorously not only the preaching of the Word but any honest contention for "the faith once delivered unto the saints." We must also never forget in our zeal to "contend for the faith" that cultists are souls for whom Christ died. While we must refute their anti-Christian teachings we must also love them as Christ commanded and seek to win them to Him. They deserve *not* our scorn but our love, that by God's grace they may reach repentance. May God in His infinite mercy and boundless grace see fit to arouse His people to the great challenge which stands at the threshold of His glorious appearing — as it is written, "Not by might, nor by power, but by my spirit, saith the Lord of Hosts."

BIBLIOGRAPHY

Cole, Marley, *Jehovah's Witnesses, The New World Society* (Vantage Press, 1955).

Further Watch Tower Bible and Tract Society publications:
   Let God Be True, revised edition, 1952.
   The New World Translation of the Hebrew Scriptures.
   Make Sure of All Things
   The Emphatic Diaglott

Martin, Walter R., and Klann, Norman H., *Jehovah of the Watchtower* (Zondervan Publishing House, 1955).

Mayer, F. E., *Jehovah's Witnesses* (Concordia Publishing House, 1943).

Russell, Charles Taze, *Studies in the Scriptures*, Vols. I-VI, (Watch Tower Bible and Tract Society).

Rutherford, J. F., *The Harp of God, Life, Light, Enemies, Salvation, Children*, etc. (Watch Tower Bible and Tract Society).

Stroup, Herbert Hewitt, *The Jehovah's Witnesses* (Columbia University Press, 1945).

The Watchtower and Awake (periodical), assorted issues (Watch Tower Bible and Tract Society).

The New World Translations of the Hebrew and Christian Scriptures (Watch Tower Bible and Tract Society).